MY FIRST
SCIENCE
B·O·O·K

ANGELA WILKES

Stoddart

Art Editor Thomas Keenes
Photography Dave King

Managing Art Editor Roger Priddy

Published in Canada in 1990 by
Stoddart Publishing Co. Limited
34 Lesmill Road
Toronto, Canada
M3B 2T6

Published in Great Britain by
Dorling Kindersley Limited
9 Henrietta Street
London

Canadian Cataloguing in Publication Data

Wilkes, Angela
My first science book

ISBN 0-7737-2435-4

I. Science – Experiments – Juvenile literature.
I. Title

Q164.W55 1990   j507′.8   C90-094355-6

Phototypeset by Bookworm Typesetting, Manchester
Reproduced in Singapore by Colourscan
Printed in Italy by LEGO

Dorling Kindersley would like to thank Penny Britchfield,
Jonathan Buckley, Amy Douglas, Nancy Graham, Steve
Parker, and Toby Spigel for their help in producing this book.

Illustrations by Brian Delf

CONTENTS

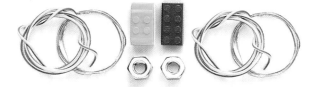

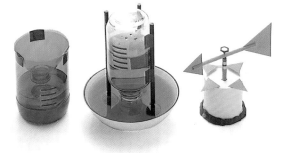

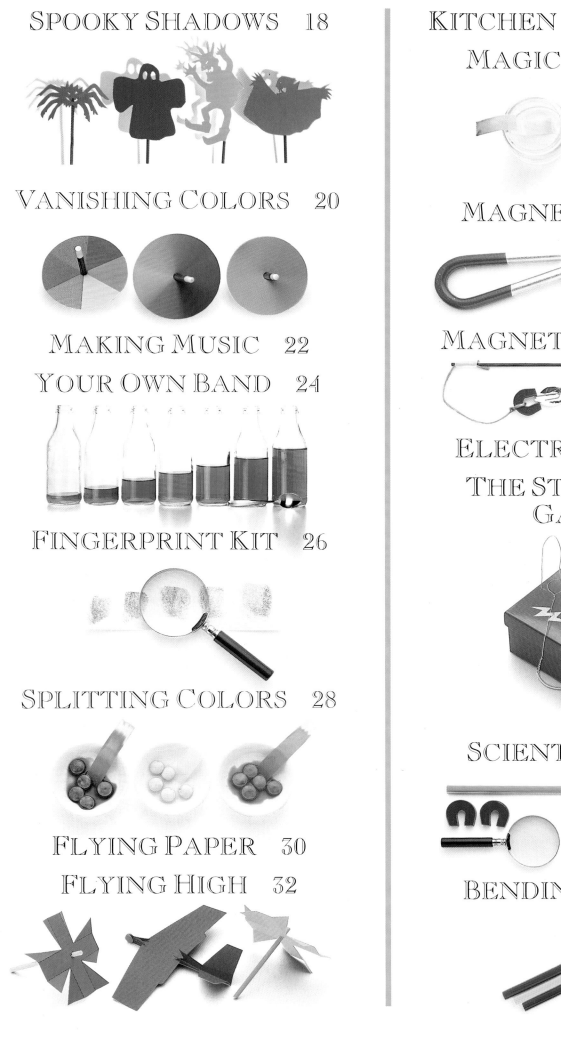

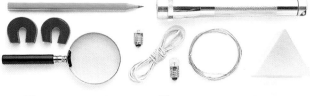

SCIENCE BY PICTURES

My First Science Book is full of fascinating experiments to do at home that will help you to find out why things happen the way they do in the world around you. Step-by-step photographs and simple instructions show you exactly what to do, and there are life-size photographs of all the materials you will need and of the finished projects. On the opposite page is a list of things to read before you start, and below are the points to look for in each project.

How to use this book

The aim of the experiment
At the beginning of each experiment you can read exactly what the experiment is setting out to do.

The things you need
The materials for each experiment are shown life-size, to help you be sure you have everything you need.

Equipment
These illustrated checklists show you which equipment to have ready before you start an experiment.

KITCHEN CHEMISTRY

You don't need special powders and test tubes to be a chemist. Everything around you is made of chemicals, and you can do all kinds of interesting tests on things around the kitchen. Here and on the next three pages you can find out how to test things to see if they are acid or alkaline.

You will need

Blotting paper

Half a lemon

Baking soda

Water

Half a small red cabbage

Other things to test

Egg white

Cola drink

Milk of magnesia

Vinegar

A hard candy

A tomato

A slice of apple

Orange juice

Yogurt

Baking powder

Washing soda*

EQUIPMENT

Chopping board

Sieve

Bowl

Teaspoon

Small glasses or jars

Pen or pencil

Knife

Jug

Sticky labels

Notebook

The acid test

1 Chop up the cabbage and put it in the bowl.* Pour hot water over it and let it soak until the water turns purple.

2 Hold the sieve over the jug. Pour the cabbage water into the jug through the sieve, so that the cabbage stays in the sieve.

3 Pour a little purple cabbage water into several of the small jars. Label one jar *Control* and put it to one side.

4 Pour a few drops of lemon juice into one of the other jars of purple cabbage water. Label the jar *Lemon juice*.

5 Mix 4ml of baking soda with a little water. Stir it into a jar of purple water. Label it *Baking soda*.

6 Do the same with all the other things you want to test. Label every jar to say what is in it as you do each test. Now turn the page.

34 *Ask an adult to help you with the knife.

*Wash your hands after handling washing soda. 35

Things to remember

1 Read the instructions before you start, and gather together everything you need for the experiment.

2 Put on an apron or an old shirt and roll up your sleeves. Cover your worktable with newspaper.

3 Follow the instructions carefully and do only one thing at a time.

4 Be very careful with needles, scissors, and batteries. Do not use them unless an adult is there to help you.

5 Keep a record of each experiment and its results in your science notebook (see page 47).

6 When you have finished, put everything away, clean up any mess, and wash your hands.

Step by step
Step-by-step photographs and clear instructions show you exactly what to do at each stage of the experiment.

Explanation
At the end of each experiment you will find a simple explanation of what has happened and why.

The final results
Life-size pictures show you what happens at the end of the experiment, so that you know what to expect.

MAGIC POTIONS

Changing color

1 Squeeze a little lemon juice into two jars. Mix 8ml of baking soda with water in a third jar.

2 Add some purple cabbage water to the two jars of lemon juice. The lemon juice should turn pink. Label one jar *Control*.

3 Add the baking soda water to one jar of pink lemon juice, drop by drop. What happens to the color of the lemon juice?

THE ACID TEST

Alkalis
If the cabbage water turns blue or green, as it does with baking soda, the thing you have tested is an alkali.

Lemon

Baking soda

Control jar
You keep the Control jar to compare with the tests you do.

Purple water with lemon juice added to it

Acids
If the purple cabbage water turns pink, as with the lemon juice, the thing you have tested is acid.

Purple water with a candy added to it

Purple water with baking soda added to it

36

The litmus test

1 Cut a piece of blotting paper into small strips about 1 cm wide.* Cut a lot of strips so that you can test several liquids.

2 Dip the strips of blotting paper into purple cabbage water, then lay them on a saucer to dry. This might take a few hours.

3 Dip a strip of paper into each liquid you want to test. Try lemon juice, then baking soda mixed with water.

CHANGING COLOR
As you add the baking soda (an alkali) to the lemon juice (an acid), the pink water turns purple. This shows that the liquid is no longer acid.

Lemon juice

Purple water with lemon juice added to it

Baking Soda

Strips of litmus paper

Pink water with baking soda added to it

THE LITMUS TEST
Scientists use litmus paper to test liquids to see if they are acid or alkaline. You can make your own. When you dip litmus paper into an acid, it turns pink. When you dip it into an alkali, it turns blue or green.

*Ask an adult to help you with the scissors. 37

MAGIC BALLOONS

Some of the most interesting science experiments help you to see the effects of invisible forces at work around you. Strange things can happen to the most ordinary everyday objects. Here you can find out how to give balloons powers that seem magical.

A sheet of paper torn into small pieces

You will need

Balloons

Sugar

What to do

1 Blow up the balloons. You may need an adult to help you do this. Tie the end of each balloon into a firm knot.

2 Now rub each balloon hard against your sweater. The tricks work best if the sweater you are wearing is made of wool.

3 Hold one balloon just above the torn-up pieces of paper. What happens? Then try holding a balloon just above some sugar.

"MAGICAL" ATTRACTION

The balloons pick up the torn-up paper and sugar, as if by magic.

Electrical charges

Rubbing a balloon against wool charges it with static electricity. This gives the balloon enough magnetic power to pick up very light things, like the paper and sugar. It also makes the paper and sugar stick to the balloon.

Most things contain static electricity. You cannot see it, but you can rub it off one thing and onto another, making it static.

7

BOTTLE VOLCANO

This simple experiment with water shows in a dramatic way exactly what happens when you mix hot liquids and cold liquids together.

You will need

String

A small bottle

A large glass jar

Red food coloring or ink

EQUIPMENT

Scissors

Paintbrush

Setting up the volcano

1 Cut a piece of string about 30 cm long.* Tie one end of it firmly around the neck of the bottle, leaving the other end free.

2 Tie the other end of the string to the piece tied around the neck of the bottle, to make a loop of string for a handle.

3 Fill the large jar with cold water. Don't fill it all the way to the top, as you will need space to lower the bottle into it.

Ask an adult to help you with the scissors.

8

4 Fill the small bottle up to the top with hot water. Stir in enough drops of food coloring to turn the water bright red.

5 Hold the small bottle by the string handle and lower it gently into the jar of cold water, being careful to keep it level.

VOLCANO IN A JAR

As you lower the small bottle into the jar of cold water, the hot water shoots up into the cold water like a volcano. Soon all the hot water will rise to the top of the jar.

Why hot water rises

When water is heated, it expands (takes up more space). This makes the hot water lighter than the cold water, so the hot water rises to the surface.

ON THE LEVEL

No two liquids are the same. Have you ever wondered why cream floats on top of milk, or why salad dressing separates into different layers? And did you know that some objects will sink in water but float on another liquid? In this experiment you can find out some fascinating things about different liquids and create a colorful giant cocktail at the same time.

Vegetable oil

You will need

EQUIPMENT

`Large spoon

Jug

Honey

Things to float

Nuts

Plastic toys

Small metal objects

Small tomatoes

Water colored with ink or food coloring

A large clear-plastic container

Dried pasta

Grapes

What to do

1 Carefully pour honey into the container over the back of the spoon, until the container is a quarter full.

2 Slowly pour the same amount of vegetable oil into the container. Then add the same amount of colored water.

3 Wait until the liquids have settled into layers. Then gently drop different objects into the container, to see what floats.

LIQUID COCKTAIL

The liquids separate into three layers, with the honey on the bottom, the water above that, and the oil on top of the water.
Liquids do this because some of them are lighter or less dense than others. A lighter liquid will float on top of a heavier or more dense liquid.

Floaters and sinkers

Some of the objects you drop into the container will sink. Others will float at different levels, depending on how heavy they are. Objects float best in dense liquids, as these support their weight best.

11

MULTICOLORED FLOWERS

Why do we put flowers in a vase of water? Where does the water in the vase go? In this clever experiment you use food coloring or ink to reveal something that you would normally never see: how flowers drink and where the water goes.

You will need

White carnations

Jug of water

Different-colored inks or food dyes

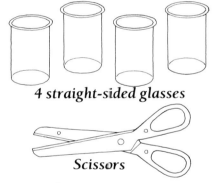

EQUIPMENT

4 straight-sided glasses

Scissors

What to do

1 Pour 2.5 cm of different-coloured food coloring or ink into each glass. Add 2.5 cm of water to each glass.

2 Trim the flower stems to 5 cm taller than the glasses.* Cut along the stems of two flowers, to split them in half lengthwise.

3 Stand a flower in each glass of water. Stand each half of the two split-stemmed flowers in different-colored water.

12

Ask an adult to help you with the scissors.

Red flower

Blue flower

Pink flower

Green flower

Tiny veins

Look closely at the flowers and you will see the tiny veins that carry water to each part of the flower petals. The veins have been stained by the food coloring.

Color change

Leave the flowers in a warm room for a few hours and they will slowly turn the same color as the water in which they are standing.

Pink and blue flower

Red and green flower

Two-tone Flowers

Each half of the flowers with the split stems will turn the same color as the water in which that half of the stem is standing. This shows that the tiny tubes for water in each part of the flower stem lead to a specific part of the flower.

13

WEATHER STATION

Set up your own weather station and keep a record of your local weather. Here and on the following pages you can find out how to make a rain gauge, for measuring rainfall; a barometer, to show changes in air pressure; and a wind vane, to tell you which way the wind is blowing.

You will need

Food coloring or ink

Waterproof tape

A glue stick

A short pencil with an eraser on the end
Three long pencils

A drinking straw

A shallow bowl

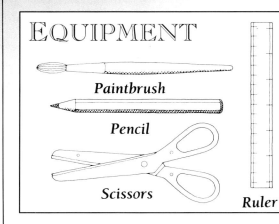

EQUIPMENT

Paintbrush

Pencil

Scissors

Ruler

A yogurt container

A large, straight-sided plastic bottle

14

Thin cardboard

A pushpin

Modeling clay

A narrow clear-plastic bottle*

* Use the narrowest bottle you can find.

Making the wind vane

1 Make a hole in the center of the base of the yogurt container. Push the short pencil into it, so the eraser end sticks out.

2 Cut four small triangles out of cardboard.** Then cut out a triangle 3 cm deep and a bigger one 5 cm deep.

3 Glue the four small triangles to the base of the yogurt container so that they point in four different directions, as shown.

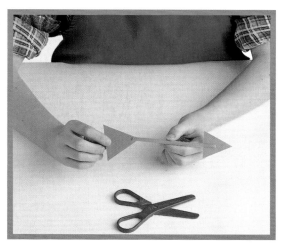

4 Cut a 1 cm slit at each end of the straw. Slot a big triangle into each slit, both pointing in the same direction.

5 Push the pin through the center of the straw.** Then stick the pin into the eraser. Make sure the vane can spin easily.

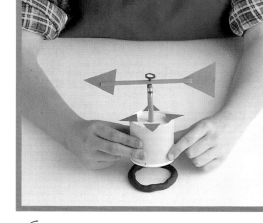

6 Make a sausage of modeling clay and bend it into a circle. Push the clay around the base of the wind vane.

** Ask an adult to help you.

15

WEATHER WATCH

Making the rain gauge

1 Cut off the top quarter of the large plastic bottle, using the scissors. Ask an adult to help you.

2 Slide the top of the bottle upside down into the base of the bottle, to act as a funnel. Tape the edges together, as shown.

3 Cut tiny strips of waterproof tape.* Tape them to the side of the bottle about 0.5 cm apart, to act as a measuring scale.

Making the barometer

1 Tape three long pencils to the small plastic bottle. The points of the pencils should stick out above the top of the bottle.

2 Using the bottle as a guide, stick three lumps of modeling clay to the bottom of the bowl. The pencils will go into them.

3 Half fill both the bowl and the bottle with water. With the paintbrush, add a few drops of food coloring or ink to the water.

4 Cover the top of the bottle with your hand. Turn it upside down and lower it under the water in the bowl.

5 Take your hand away from the mouth of the bottle. Keeping the bottle straight, push the pencils firmly into the modeling clay.

6 Cut tiny strips of tape.* Tape them to the side of the bottle to make a scale, as with the rain gauge.

16

Ask an adult to help you.

RECORDING THE WEATHER

Stand your wind vane and rain gauge outside. Keep the barometer indoors, away from direct sunlight. Check your weather station every day and make a record in your science notebook of any changes. As well as reading the instruments you have made, write down how many hours of rain or sun there have been and note what kinds of clouds are in the sky.

How the barometer works

A barometer measures air pressure. Air presses down on the water in the bowl. When the air pressure rises, the air pushes down harder on the water, making the water in the bottle rise higher up the scale. When the air pressure drops, the water level in the bottle drops lower.

The water level will rise or drop only slightly, so check it very carefully.

If your rain gauge has a plastic base, fill the base with water before putting the rain gauge outside.

Measuring the rainfall

When it rains, check how far up the scale the water comes every day. Make a note of the reading, then empty the rain gauge.

Which way is the wind blowing?

Stand the wind vane outside on a flat surface. Use a compass to position it so that one of the triangles points north. Mark the triangles north, south, east, and west. Write down which direction the wind is blowing from. A north wind, for example, blows from north to south.

17

SPOOKY SHADOWS

Make some scary puppets and treat your friends to a spine-chilling shadow puppet show. Below are some puppet patterns to trace, and opposite you can see how to make and operate the puppets.

Tracing paper

You will need

Thin cardboard

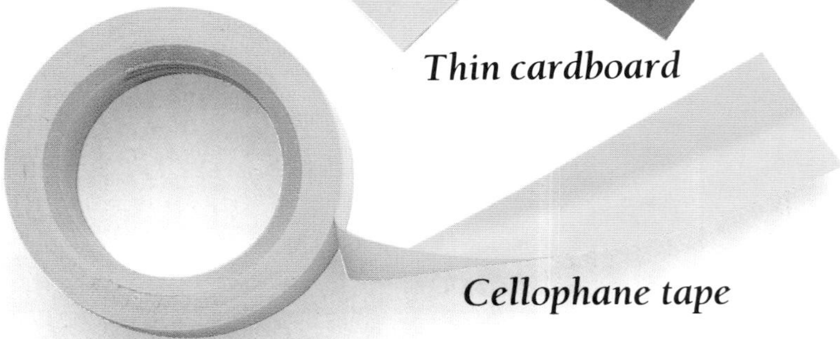

Thin sticks

Cellophane tape

EQUIPMENT

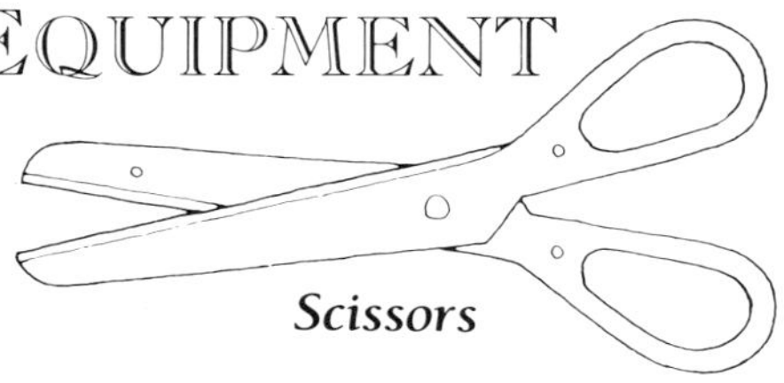

Scissors

Pencil

A strong flashlight

Puppet patterns

Vicious vampire

Terrifying tarantula

Scary specter

Ghastly ghoul

18

Making the puppets

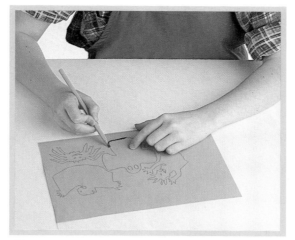

1 Trace the puppet patterns on tracing paper. (Or make up your own puppets and draw them straight on cardboard.)

2 Lay the tracing paper wrong side down on cardboard. Scribble over the back of the traced lines, to transfer them to cardboard.

3 Carefully cut the puppets out of the cardboard.* Use a pencil to make holes for eyes. Tape each puppet to the end of a stick.

SHADOW THEATER

You need two people to set up the theater: one to hold the flashlight and the other to work the puppets. Make sure the room is dark, then shine the flashlight at the wall and move the puppets around between the flashlight and the wall. With practice, you can make the shadows grow bigger and even change shape.

Monster shadows

Light rays are straight. So the closer a puppet is to the flashlight, the more light it blocks and the bigger the shadow.

*Ask an adult to help you.

19

VANISHING COLORS

Light looks white, but it is really made of rainbow colors. With this simple multicolored wheel you will be able to make colors disappear, then appear again, as if by magic. Where do the colors go and why? Spin the wheel, then read about what happens at the bottom of the opposite page.

You will need

Thin cardboard

A short, sharp pencil

Tracing paper

A glue stick

Colored paper (red, orange, yellow, green, blue, and purple)

Making the color wheel

1 Open compass to 5 cm.* Draw a circle on the cardboard. Then mark six points, 5 cm apart, around the circle, with compass.

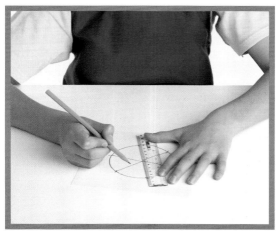

2 Draw a line between each pair of opposite points, so the three lines cross in the center of the circle. Cut out the circle.**

20

*A compass point is very sharp. Ask an adult to help you.

**Ask an adult to help you with the scissors.

3 Trace a segment of the circle. Glue it onto cardboard and cut it out. Trace the shape on each color of paper and cut it out.

4 Glue the pieces of colored paper to cardboard circle in this order: red, orange, yellow, green, blue, and purple.

5 Punch a hole in the center of the circle with the tip of the scissors.** Push the pencil through the hole, as shown.

SPINNING COLORS

Holding the eraser end of the pencil, spin the color wheel fast and watch what happens. Which color or colors can you see? When the wheel spins fast, your eyes and brain working together cannot see each color separately, so the colors blur together to make a different color.

As the color wheel slows down, the blurring lessens, and your eyes and brain can pick out the different colors again. Try making other wheels in just two or three colors. Do you always see the same color when you spin them?

21

MAKING MUSIC

Why do things make sounds? Sound is around you all the time, but you cannot see it. Try making your own musical instruments, though, and you will not only have lots of fun, but will also learn about how sounds are made. Here you can find out how to make a harp from rubber bands, a xylophone from bottles, and panpipes from drinking straws. Turn the page to see the finished instruments, then start twanging, banging, and blowing!

A glue stick

You will need

8 plastic drinking straws

A metal spoon

Water

Food coloring or ink

Several glass bottles the same size

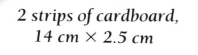

2 strips of cardboard,
14 cm × 2.5 cm

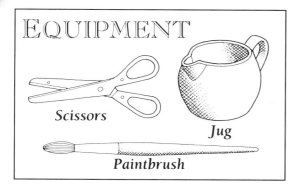

Thick rubber
bands

A baking tin
or plastic box

Making the panpipes

1 Spread glue along one cardboard strip. Glue the eight straws to the cardboard at equal distances, with tops of straws in line.

2 Glue the second strip of cardboard over top of straws. Trim the straws so that each one is shorter than the one next to it.*

Making the harp

1 Stretch eight rubber bands around the baking tin or plastic box as shown, so that they are all the same distance apart.

2 To give the rubber bands different notes, tighten each one by pulling it and catching it on the edge of the tin or box.

Making the xylophone

1 Stand the bottles in a row. Pour water into them, so that each bottle contains a little more water than the one next to it.

2 To make the xylophone look prettier, add a few drops of food coloring to each bottle of water and stir it in.

*Ask an adult to help you with the scissors.

YOUR OWN BAND

Now that you have made your musical instruments, see if you can play a tune on any of them. The instruments shown here are plucked, blown, and banged on, but each of them really makes sounds in the same way. All sounds, both nice and nasty, are carried by the air around you. When you play a musical instrument, it makes the air around it vibrate. The air carries this vibration to your ears. Your eardrums then vibrate, and you hear the sound made by the instrument.

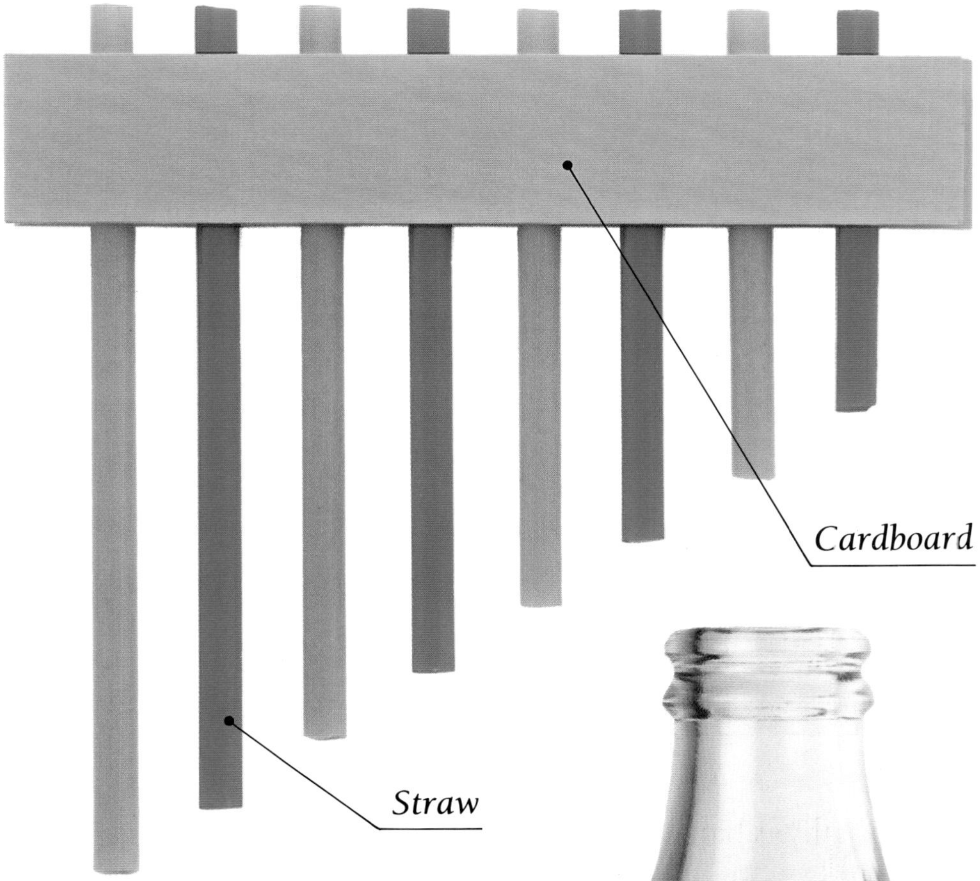

Cardboard

Straw

PANPIPES

The pipes are a simple wind instrument. Hold them to your mouth with the straws pointing downward, as shown here, and blow across the tops of the straws. You will hear quiet, flute-like sounds. The shorter the straws are, the higher the notes they make.

BOTTLE XYLOPHONE

The xylophone forms the percussion part of your band. Tap each bottle in turn with the spoon to see what note it makes. The more water there is in the bottle, the shorter the column of air that vibrates in the bottle and the higher the sound it makes.

If you adjust the amount of water in the bottles, you should find that you can play part of a musical scale by striking each one in turn.

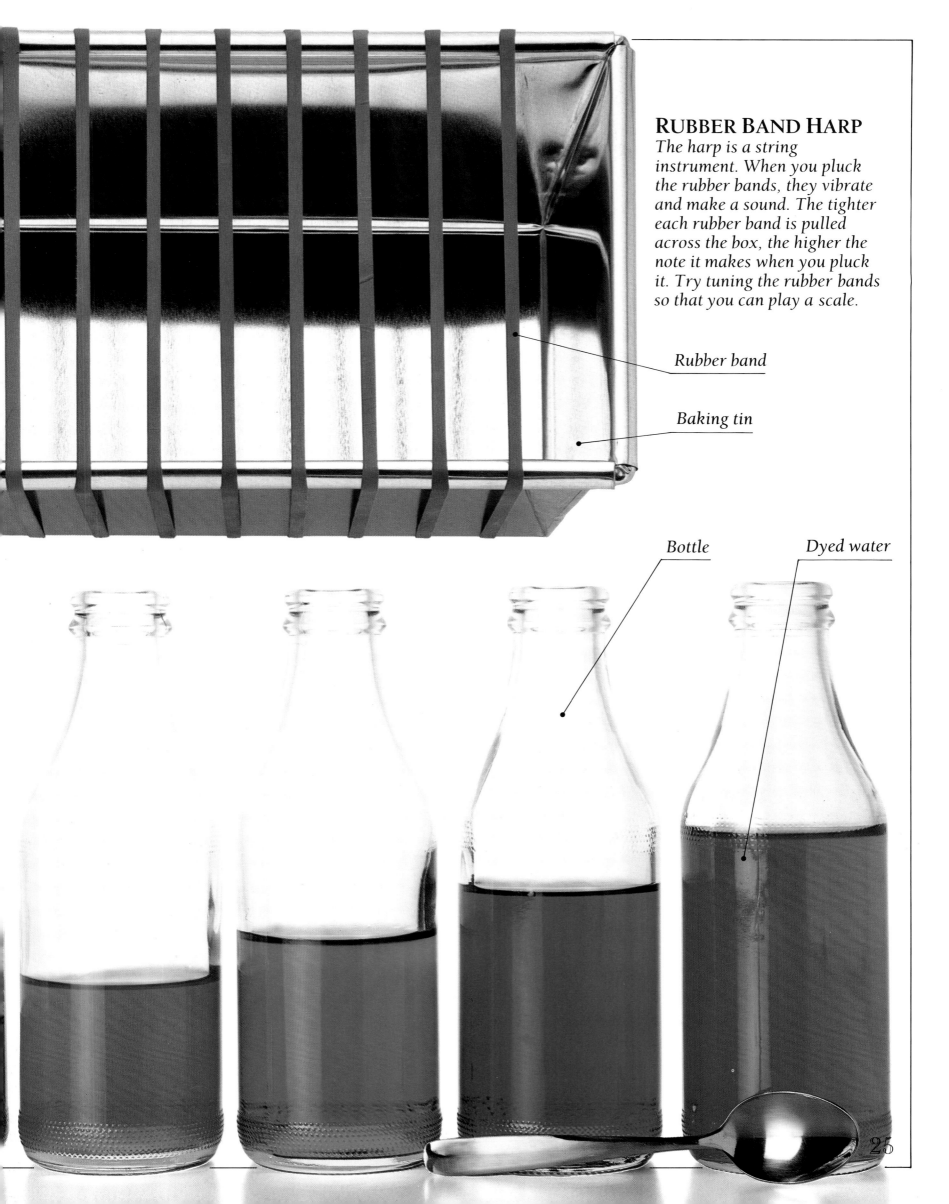

RUBBER BAND HARP

The harp is a string instrument. When you pluck the rubber bands, they vibrate and make a sound. The tighter each rubber band is pulled across the box, the higher the note it makes when you pluck it. Try tuning the rubber bands so that you can play a scale.

Rubber band

Baking tin

Bottle

Dyed water

FINGERPRINT KIT

No two people have the same fingerprints. This makes fingerprints valuable clues when detectives are investigating a crime. Fingerprints are usually invisible, but detectives use scientific methods to reveal prints found at the scene of a crime and compare them with suspects' fingerprints. Read the directions below and do some detective work of your own.

You will need

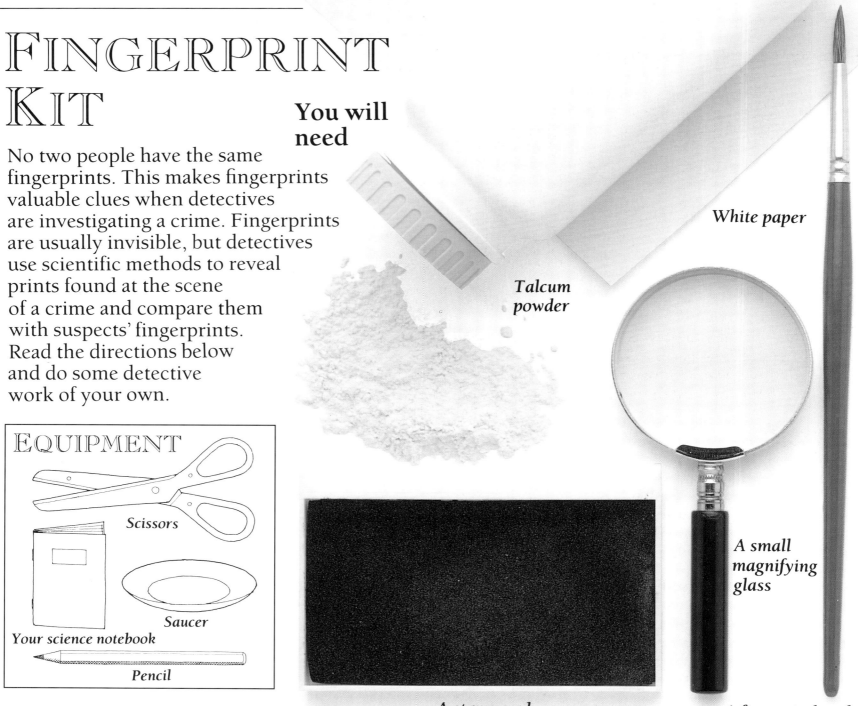

Talcum powder

White paper

A small magnifying glass

A stamp pad

A fine paintbrush

EQUIPMENT

Scissors

Your science notebook

Saucer

Pencil

Taking fingerprints

1 Press the pad of one of the suspect's fingers lightly on the stamp pad. Roll it from side to side, to cover it with ink.

2 Press the suspect's finger firmly on a piece of paper. Hold it as shown in the picture and roll it from side to side.

3 Take prints of each of the suspect's fingers and label them. Then examine them carefully. Are all the prints the same?

* The edges of windows, door knobs and light switches are good places to try.

Dusting for fingerprints

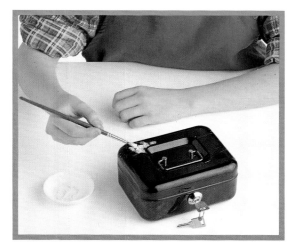

1 Pour some talcum powder into a saucer. Dust the talcum powder lightly on something hard and shiny that people often touch*.

2 Blow gently on the places that you have powdered. Most of the powder will blow away, except where there are greasy marks.

3 Now brush the powdered spots very lightly with a fine paintbrush. Any fingerprints will gradually appear, as if by magic.

FINGERPRINT FILE

When you have taken all the suspects' fingerprints, cut them out and glue them into your science notebook.** Then you can compare them with any fingerprints you find around your home.

Use a magnifying glass to study the details of fingerprints.

Suspect's fingerprint

Fingerprint found on cash box

**Ask an adult to help you with the scissors.

SPLITTING COLORS

Many of the inks and dyes that are used to color things are really mixtures of several different-colored chemicals or *pigments*. The two experiments here show you how to separate the different-colored pigments in felt-tip pens and in the food coloring used in candy.

EQUIPMENT

Glass or jelly jar   Jug of water

Scissors

Saucers

You will need

Colored felt-tip pens

White blotting paper

2ml of salt

Candy-covered chocolates

Felt-tip pen test

1 Cut out a rectangle of blotting paper big enough to roll into a tube that you can slide into the glass you are going to use.*

2 With the felt-tip pens, make blobs of different colors** about 4 cm from the bottom of the blotting paper.

3 Pour a little water into the glass and stir in the salt. Roll the blotting paper into a tube and stand it in the glass.

28

Ask an adult to help you with the scissors.

Candy test

1 Choose three colors to test. Put five or six candies the same color in each saucer. Add a few drops of water to each saucer.

2 Turn the candies over and stir them around a little, so that most of the color runs off them and colors the water.

3 Cut three strips of blotting paper.* Lay a strip in each of the saucers as shown, with one end in the colored water.

**Dark colors are the most interesting to test.

FELT-TIP PEN TEST

As the water rises up the blotting paper, it dissolves the pigments in the ink blots and carries them up with it. The different pigments move up the paper at different speeds, so they separate and you can see bands of different colors.

CANDY TEST

The pigments used on the candy are absorbed by the blotting paper in the same way as the pigments in the felt-tip pens. As they move up the blotting paper, they separate. Some of the colors contain only one pigment.

FLYING PAPER

How do airplanes fly? Launch a piece of paper into the air and it will just flutter to the ground. But if you make a plane with the piece of paper, it will fly really well.

Here and on the next three pages you can find out how to make an amazing superglider and a helicopter. They are not only fun to make and play with, but will also teach you a lot about how things fly.

You will need

Spool of thread

Thin cardboard

A paper clip

A glue stick

A drinking straw 20 cm long

Tracing paper

A small lump of modeling clay

String

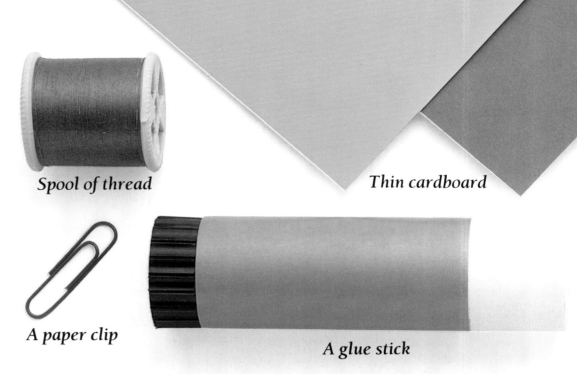

HELICOPTER PATTERN

Fold up   *Fold down*

Fold down   *Fold up*

Fold up   *Fold down*

Fold down   *Fold up*

EQUIPMENT

Scissors

Ruler   *Pencil*

SUPERGLIDER PATTERN

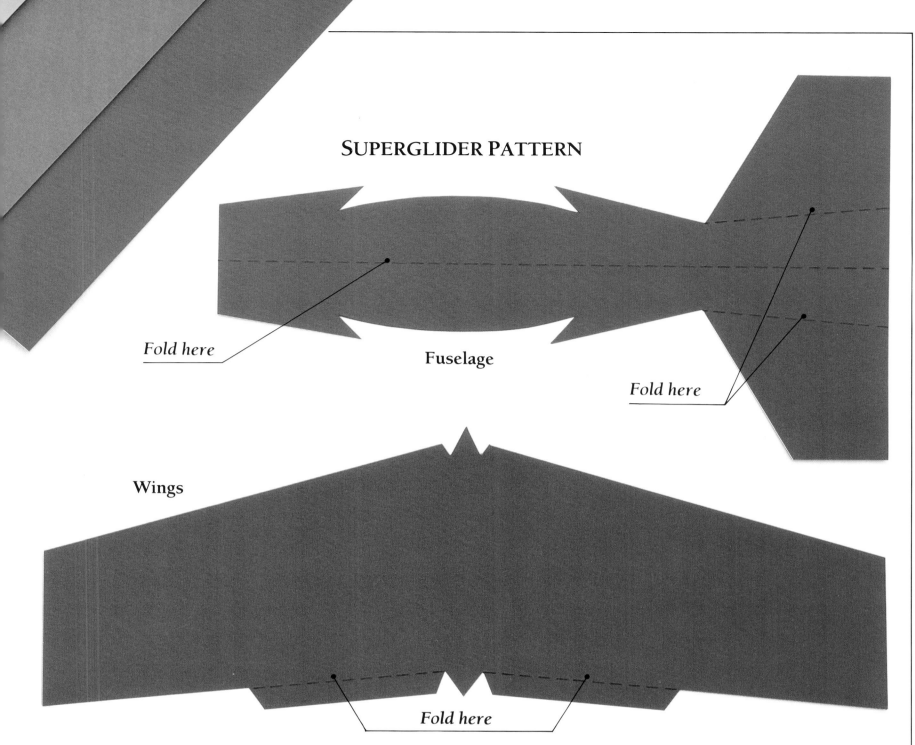

Fold here

Fuselage

Fold here

Wings

Fold here

Making the superglider

1 Trace the outlines of the two superglider pattern pieces on tracing paper. Trace along the fold lines, using dotted lines.

2 Turn the tracing paper over. Lay it on cardboard and scribble over the lines you have traced, to transfer pattern to cardboard.

3 Cut wings and fuselage out of cardboard.* Score along the fold lines, using your ruler and the point of your scissors.**

*Ask an adult to help you with the scissors.   **This helps to make the folds sharper.

Now turn the page.

FLYING HIGH

Superglider (continued)

4 Fold the fuselage in half along the fold line, then open it out again. Fold down the two tail fins and the two wing flaps.

5 Slot the back of the wings into the back notches on the fuselage. Slot the front of the wings into the front two notches.

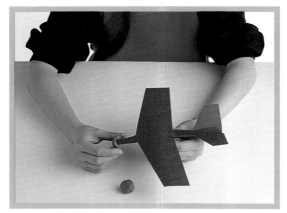

6 Put the paper clip on the nose of the airplane. Fold a piece of modeling clay around the paper clip, to act as a weight.

Making the helicopter

1 Trace the pattern for the helicopter rotor on tracing paper. Trace the fold lines, using dotted lines.

2 Turn the tracing paper over. Lay it on cardboard and scribble over the lines you have traced, to transfer pattern to cardboard.

3 Cut the helicopter rotor out of cardboard.* Score along the fold lines, using your ruler and the point of your scissors.**

4 Each rotor blade has two fold lines. Fold one side of each rotor blade up and the other side down, along the fold lines.

5 Make a hole in the middle of the rotor.* Spread glue around one end of the straw. Push the straw through the hole in the rotor.

6 Make a loop in one end of the string. Wind string counter-clockwise over the loop around the straw beneath the rotor.

*Ask an adult to help you.   **This helps to make the folds sharper.

Helicopter launch

Push the straw into the spool of thread. Hold the spool in one hand and pull the string hard with the other.

As the helicopter rotors spin, they push air down, squashing the air under the rotors. The pressure of this air pushes the helicopter into the air.

Taking off

To launch the superglider, hold it just behind the nose and let it go gently. The plane flies because the shape of the wings makes the air flow faster over the wings than below them. The pressure of air below the wing is greater than it is above the wing, helping to push the plane up and keep it in the air.

If the superglider keeps tipping upward and then diving, try adding a little more modeling clay to the nose. If the glider dives too fast, the nose may be too heavy, so remove some modeling clay.

33

KITCHEN CHEMISTRY

You don't need special powders and test tubes to be a chemist. Everything around you is made of chemicals, and you can do all kinds of interesting tests on things around the kitchen. Here and on the next three pages you can find out how to test things to see if they are acid or alkaline.

Blotting paper

Half a lemon

You will need

Baking soda

Water

Half a small red cabbage

The acid test

1 Chop up the cabbage and put it in the bowl.* Pour hot water over it and let it soak until the water turns purple.

2 Hold the sieve over the jug. Pour the cabbage water into the jug through the sieve, so that the cabbage stays in the sieve.

3 Pour a little purple cabbage water into several of the small jars. Label one jar *Control* and put it to one side.

Ask an adult to help you with the knife.

Other things to test

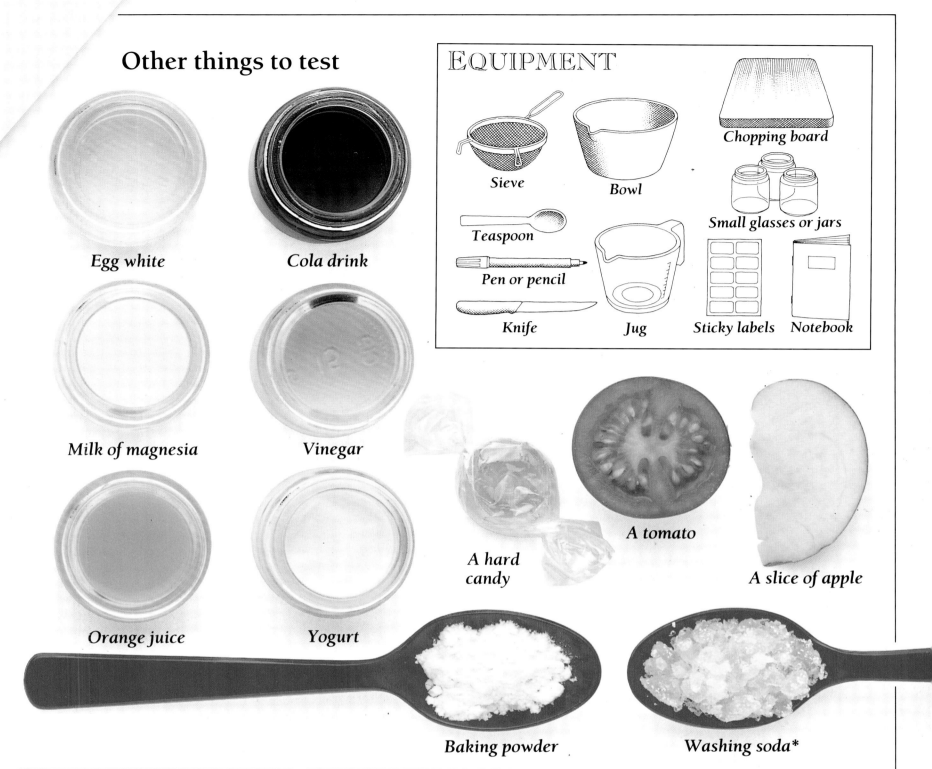

Egg white

Cola drink

Milk of magnesia

Vinegar

Orange juice

Yogurt

EQUIPMENT

Sieve

Bowl

Chopping board

Teaspoon

Small glasses or jars

Pen or pencil

Knife

Jug

Sticky labels

Notebook

A hard candy

A tomato

A slice of apple

Baking powder

Washing soda*

4 Pour a few drops of lemon juice into one of the other jars of purple cabbage water. Label the jar *Lemon juice.*

5 Mix 4ml of baking soda with a little water. Stir it into a jar of purple water. Label it *Baking soda.*

6 Do the same with all the other things you want to test. Label every jar to say what is in it as you do each test. Now turn the page.

Wash your hands after handling washing soda.

MAGIC POTIONS

Changing color

1 Squeeze a little lemon juice into two jars. Mix 8ml of baking soda with water in a third jar.

2 Add some purple cabbage water to the two jars of lemon juice. The lemon juice should turn pink. Label one jar *Control.*

3 Add the baking-soda water to one jar of pink lemon juice, drop by drop. What happens to the color of the lemon juice?

THE ACID TEST

Alkalis

If the cabbage water turns blue or green, as it does with baking soda, the thing you have tested is an alkali.

Lemon

Baking soda

Control jar
You keep the Control jar to compare with the tests you do.

Purple water with lemon juice added to it

Acids
If the purple cabbage water turns pink, as with the lemon juice, the thing you have tested is acid.

Purple water with a candy added to it

Purple water with baking soda added to it

36

The litmus test

1 Cut a piece of blotting paper into small strips about 1 cm wide.* Cut a lot of strips so that you can test several liquids.

2 Dip the strips of blotting paper into purple cabbage water, then lay them on a saucer to dry. This might take a few hours.

3 Dip a strip of paper into each liquid you want to test. Try lemon juice, then baking soda mixed with water.

CHANGING COLOR

As you add the baking soda (an alkali) to the lemon juice (an acid), the pink water turns purple. This shows that the liquid is no longer acid.

Purple water with lemon juice added to it

Lemon juice

Baking Soda

Pink water with baking soda added to it

Strips of litmus paper

THE LITMUS TEST

Scientists·use litmus paper to test liquids to see if they are acid or alkaline. You can make your own. When you dip litmus paper into an acid, it turns pink. When you dip it into an alkali, it turns blue or green.

MAGNET TRICKS

Magnets have strange powers and can draw some things to them as if by magic. You cannot see how a magnet works, but you can discover more about it by trying out the magnet tests and tricks shown here. Then turn the page to see how to set up a clever magnet game.

You will need

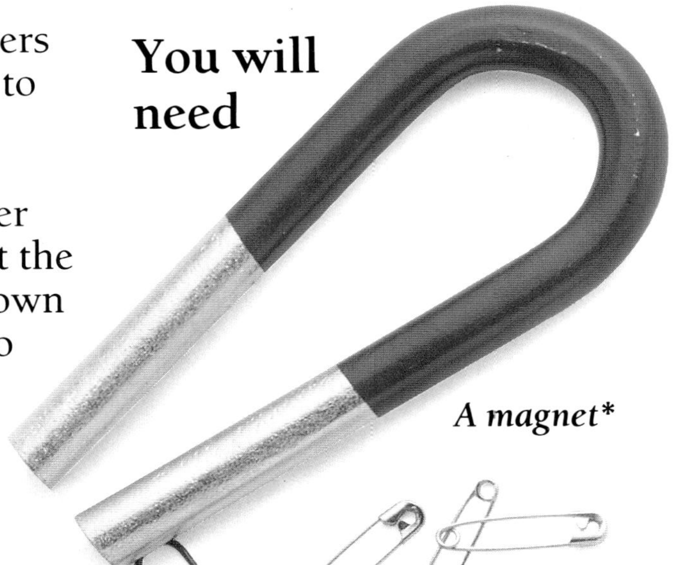

A magnet*

For the magnet tests

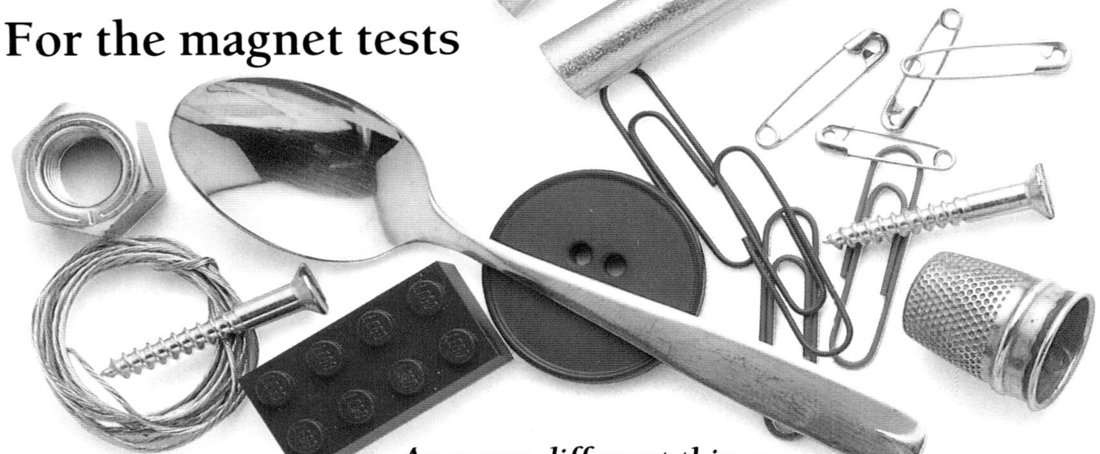

As many different things from around the home as possible

For the compass and floating needles

Small pieces of paper

2 large needles

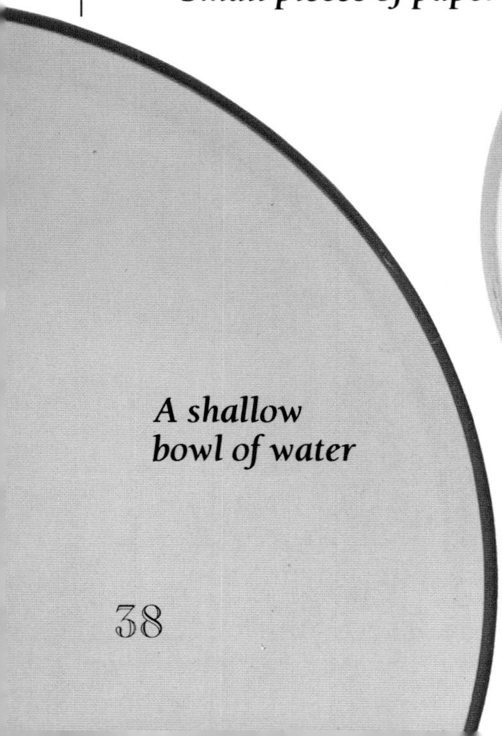

A shallow bowl of water

A glass of water

*You can buy magnets at a hardware store.

Magnet tests

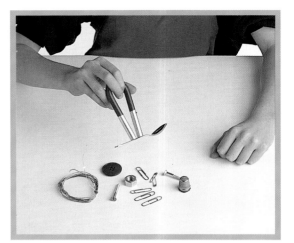

1 Test your magnet on things around the room and the objects you have collected. Which things does the magnet pick up?

2 How strong is your magnet? How many paper clips can it pick up? Can you pick them up by holding the magnet above them?

3 Do magnets work through glass? Drop a paper clip in a glass of water. Can you slide it up the glass with a magnet?

Making magnets

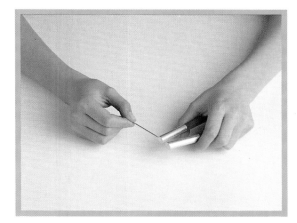

You can turn a needle into a magnet. Just stroke it about twenty times in the same direction with one end of your magnet.*

Making a compass

Magnetize a needle,* as shown above. Float a small piece of paper on water in a glass and lay the needle on top of it.

Pushing and pulling

Magnetize two needles* and lay them close together on pieces of paper floating in a bowl of water. What happens?

Finding north

The piece of paper turns until one end of the needle points north. Earth is like a giant magnet, and the magnetized needle acts like a compass needle.

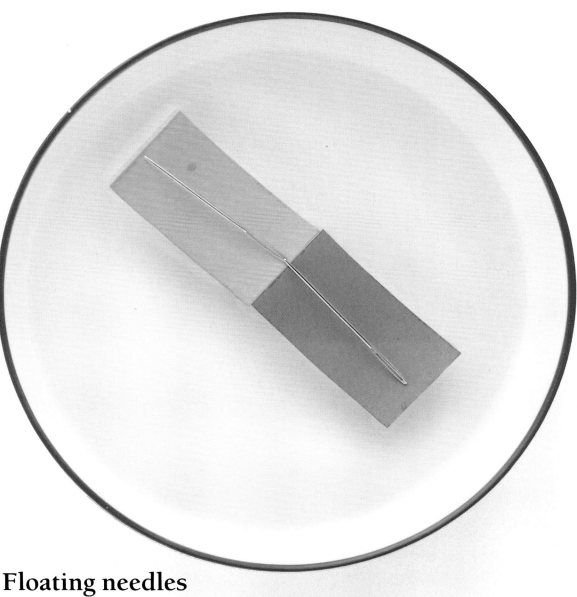

Floating needles

The pieces of paper turn as two ends of the magnetic needles pull toward each other. The two ends of a magnet are different. One end pulls one end of another magnet to it, but pushes away the other end of that same magnet.

*Be careful with the sharp end of the needle. Ask an adult to help you.

MAGNETIC FISHING

Set up this unusual fishing game and compete with your friends to see who has the mightiest magnet and can catch the most fish in the shortest time. You need a magnet for each player,* so the more magnets you have, the more people can play the game.

You will need

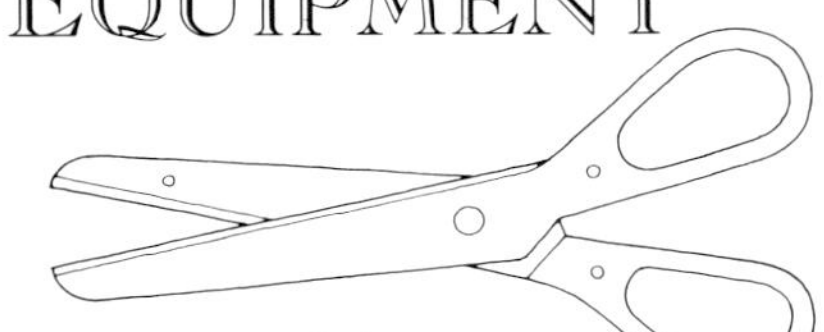

A magnet for each person playing

Lots of paper clips

Cellophane tape

EQUIPMENT

Scissors

String

A small stick for each player

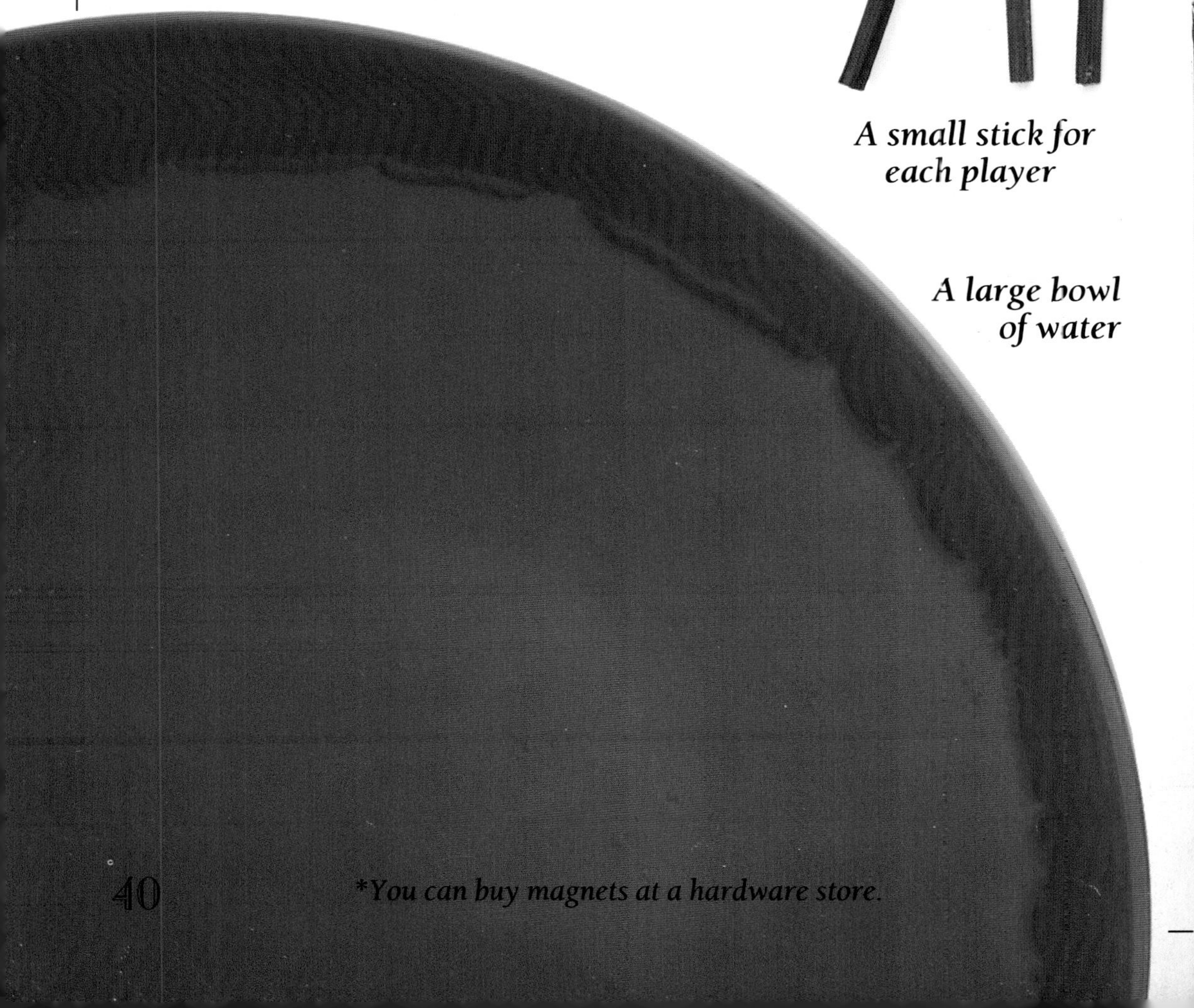

A large bowl of water

Aluminum foil

You can buy magnets at a hardware store.

Setting up the game

1 Fold the aluminum foil in half, then in half again. Cut fishes out of the folded foil, using the first fish as a pattern piece.*

2 Slide a paper clip onto the front end of each aluminum foil fish. Drop all the fish into the bowl of water.

3 Cut pieces of string about 20 cm long. Tie a magnet to one end of each piece. Tie the other end to a stick and tape it down.

How to play

Catch the fish by picking them up with the magnets. If two players catch the same fish, they must put it back in the bowl. The player who catches the most fish is the winner.

*Ask an adult to help you with the scissors.

ELECTRICAL FUN

Electricity is one of the most mysterious sources of power, yet it runs the lights in your home and many everyday household machines. The electricity that runs through wires is called current electricity. You can find out more about how it works by making a simple circuit run on a battery, which provides a small, safe amount of electricity. Below you can see how to make the circuit, and the next page will show you how to turn a circuit into a good game.

★*Electricity is very dangerous.*
   Never touch or play with electric plugs, sockets, heaters, or machines.

You will need
For the simple circuit*

A 3.5 volt bulb
and a bulb holder**

For the steady
hand game*

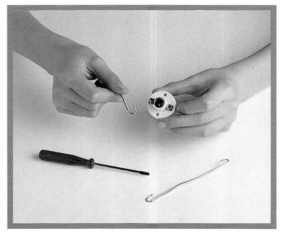

30 amp
fuse wire**

A 4.5 volt battery**

2 short pieces
of flex (insulated
electrical wire)**

Making a simple circuit

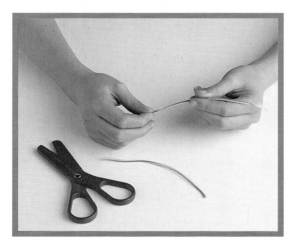

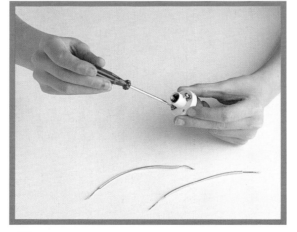

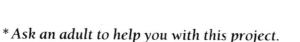

1 With an adult's help, cut 2.5 cm of plastic from each end of the two pieces of flex. Twist the little wires together to make the ends neat.

2 Loosen the screws of the bulb holder slightly, by slotting the screwdriver into them and turning it counterclockwise.

3 Make a small hook at one end of each piece of flex. Then hook a piece of flex around each screw of the bulb holder.

Ask an adult to help you with this project.   **Available in hardware stores.*

Cellophane tape

A cardboard box with a lid

A 3.5 volt bulb **

A bulb holder **

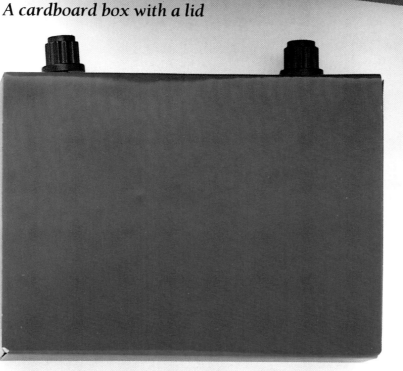

A 4.5 volt battery **

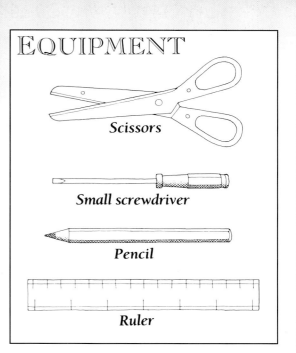

EQUIPMENT

Scissors

Small screwdriver

Pencil

Ruler

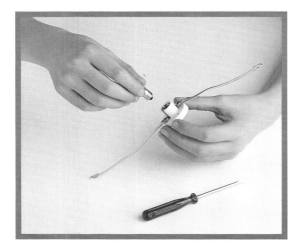

4 Tighten both screws, by slotting the screwdriver into them and turning it clockwise. Screw the bulb into the holder.

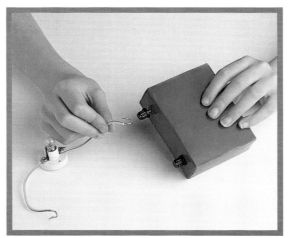

5 Loosen the small knobs on top of the battery (the terminals). Hook the end of one piece of flex onto a terminal and tighten it.

6 Hook the end of the other piece of flex onto the second terminal. The light will go on. To keep it on, tighten the terminal.

43

THE STEADY HAND GAME

What to do

1 Cut a piece of fuse wire 40 cm long and another 15 cm long.* Make a loop at one end of the short wire. Bend the long wire as shown.

2 Thread the wavy wire through the loop. Make two holes in the box lid with a pencil. Push the ends of the wire through them.

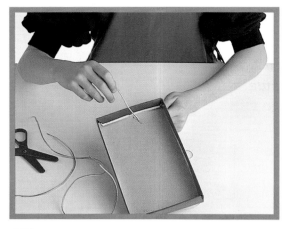

3 Cut two pieces of flex 20 cm long and another one 55 cm long. Strip the ends. Join one end of a 20 cm piece to the wavy wire.

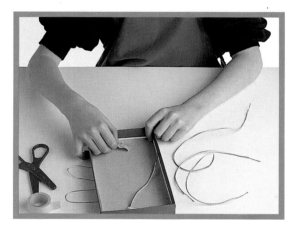

4 Tape the joined flex and wire to the inside of the box lid. Tape the other end of the wavy wire to the inside of the lid.

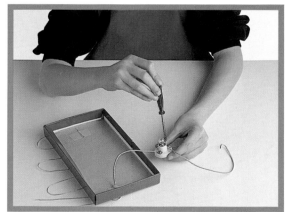

5 Screw the bulb into the bulb holder. Attach the two 20 cm pieces of flex to the bulb holder, as shown on page 42.

6 Make a small hole in the middle of the box lid.* Push the bulb up through it. Tape the bulb holder to the inside of the lid.

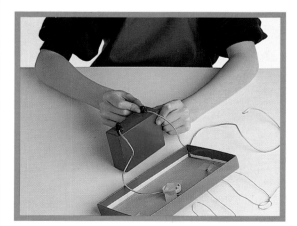

7 Attach the free end of flex from the bulb holder to the battery. Attach one end of the long piece of flex to the other terminal.

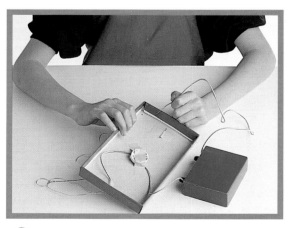

8 Make a small hole in one corner of the box lid with a pencil. Push the free end of the long flex up through it.

9 Put the battery in the box. Join the end of the wire loop to the end of the long piece of flex. Put the lid on the box.

Ask an adult to help you.

THE STEADY HAND GAME

Each person has to try and pass the loop all the way along the bent wire without touching it and making the light go on.

The more bends you make in the wire, the harder the game is to play.

Once you have made the game, you can decorate the box with shapes cut out of aluminum foil.

SIMPLE CIRCUIT

The light goes on when everything is joined together to make a circuit (a complete circle for electricity to go around). Electricity runs from the battery to the bulb, then back to the battery. If you unhook a flex from the battery, the circuit is broken and the light goes out.

45

SCIENTIST'S KIT

You do not need special equipment like test tubes to do your science experiments. You can find most of the things you need at home. Start collecting useful equipment and keep it in a special box or cupboard. Here are some of the most useful things to have in your kit.

Glue stick

Food coloring or ink, for water experiments

Cellophane tape

Jars of all sizes, for doing experiments with liquids

String

Flashlight, for experiments with light

4.5 volt batteries. You can buy these in hardware stores and hobby shops.

A funnel, for water experiments

A small magnifying glass

Horseshoe magnets, available
in hardware stores

3.5 volt bulbs, also available
in hardware stores

Bulb holders for the bulbs
shown above

Flex and fuse wire,
available in hardware
stores

A prism, for experiments
with light. You can buy one
in a toy store.

Paper towels, for
cleaning up things
you spill

Scissors

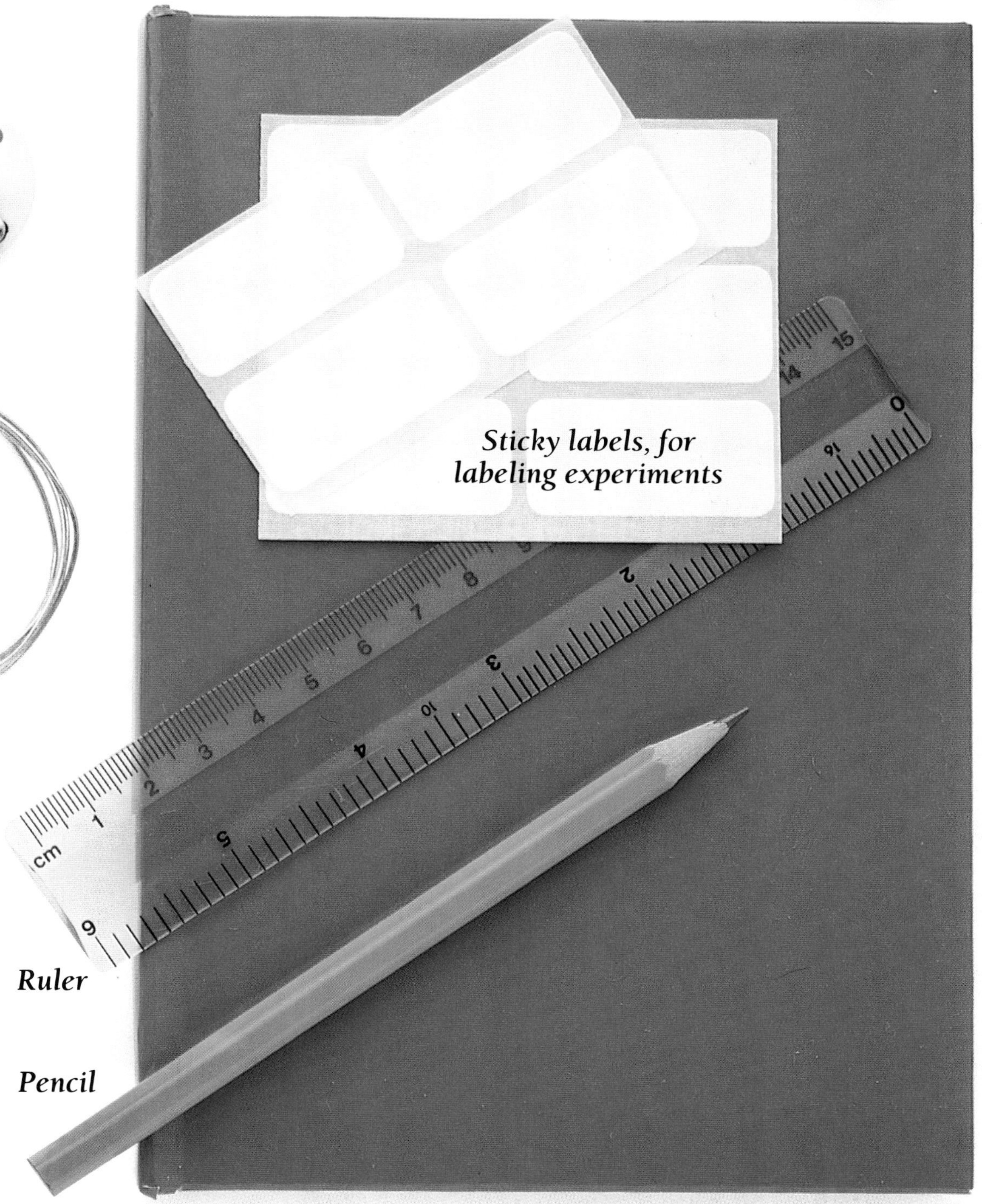

Sticky labels, for
labeling experiments

Ruler

Pencil

Science notebook, for keeping a record of
all your experiments and their results

BENDING LIGHT

Light always shines in straight lines. If you shine a flashlight in a dark room, you see a straight beam. If you block part of the beam with an object, you see a shadow, because light cannot bend around things. Sometimes, though, light does seem to bend, as these two quick experiments show.

A prism

A glass of water

Some drinking straws

What to do

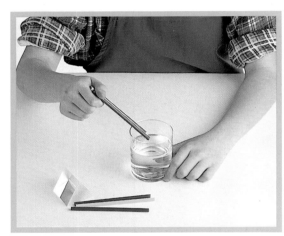

Put some straws on a table and lay the prism on top. Then stand some straws in the glass of water and look at them from the side.

Why does it happen?

Light travels fastest through air. When it enters glass or water, it slows down and changes direction a little, making things look as if they bend.

Bent straws

The straws beneath the prism look as if they are bent in two places, and the straws in the glass of water appear to bend as they enter the water.

48